THE STRUGGLE FOR MEN'S HEARTS AND MINDS

CHARLES COLSON

VICTOR BOOKS a division of SP Publications, Inc.
WHEATON, ILLINOIS 60187

Offices also in
Whitby, Ontario, Canada
Amersham-on-the-Hill, Bucks, England

Prison Fellowship Ministries
P.O. Box 17500
Washington, D.C. 20041

Second printing, 1986

The Struggle for Men's Hearts and Minds is based on Charles Colson's speech at the Christian Booksellers Association convention, Washington, D.C., July 1983.

All Scripture quotations are from the *New American Standard Bible,* © 1960, 1962, 1963, 1968, 1971, 1972, 1973, 1975, 1977 by the Lockman Foundation.

Back cover photography by David Singer.

Recommended Dewey Decimal Classification: 269
Suggested Subject Heading: SPIRITUAL RENEWAL
ISBN: 0-89693-166-8

VICTOR BOOKS
A division of SP Publications, Inc.
          Wheaton, Illinois 60187

The

CHALLENGING THE CHURCH
Series
by
CHARLES COLSON

Dare to Be Different, Dare to Be Christian

Presenting Belief in an Age of Unbelief

The Role of the Church in Society

The Struggle for Men's Hearts and Minds

We live in a time that would seem to be marked by unprecedented spiritual resurgence: 96 percent of all Americans say they believe in God; 80 percent profess to be Christians.

Yet families are splitting apart in record numbers. Countless millions of unborn children have been murdered since 1973. And there are 100 times more burglaries in so-called "Christian" America than in so-called "pagan" Japan.

Why this paradox between profession and practice? Why is the faith of more than 50 million Americans who claim to be born again not making more of an impact on the moral values of our land?

The answer is what Dietrich Bonhoeffer, the German pastor martyred by the Nazis, labeled cheap grace: the perception that Christianity offers only a flood of blessings, the rights of the kingdom without responsibilities to the King. This easy believism fails to take biblical truth to heart and fails to act in obedience to the Scriptures. The result is a church which increasingly accommodates secular values. Not knowingly, of course, but simply by gradual acceptance of secular standards which have become comfortable.

We needn't fear a sinister conspiracy to impose atheism on our society. Though such forces may be at work, they will fail precisely because they are overt.

No, the real peril today comes from the subtle ways in which the mind of our culture is being gradually won over to secular values—in the media, in classrooms, and tragically, even in our church pews. This threat is all the more insidious because it is unseen. It is the cancer of compromise.

God is calling His people today to challenge secular values, measuring them in the light of biblical revelation. Will we cave in to a culture which in principle and practice denies Christ's lordship, or will we heed His call and stand for Him?

Doing so will put us in sharp conflict with much of what the world exalts, but that must be our witness. Two centuries ago, John Wesley wrote, "Making an open stand against all ungodliness and unrighteousness, which overspreads our land as a flood, is one of the noblest ways of confessing Christ in the face of His enemies."

I can think of no more timely challenge for the Christian church today.

THE STRUGGLE FOR MEN'S HEARTS AND MINDS

~

History, in the words of a renowned French sociologist, is but "the visible effects of invisible changes in human thought." There is a profound truth here, one easily obscured by the institutionalized technocracy of the 20th century. The illusion reigns that technicians at the controls of omniscient computers, or faceless but powerful government bureaucrats, dictate our common destiny.

But in reality history is shaped, as Leo Tolstoy said, by the passions of the masses—the dreams, visions, and great ideas that seize the hearts and minds of man. As we Christians should be the first to understand, the great dialectic of history is spiritual. We are in the center of a battle for the values by which man is to live.

What are the "visible effects" of this great struggle for the hearts and minds of men? As I assess the battle, two striking images come to mind.

The first is that extraordinary scene captured on television of more than a million Poles assembled for mass in Warsaw during Pope John Paul's June 1983 visit. Though surrounded by Soviet divisions and infiltrated by the KGB, multitudes—chanting, singing, and praying—raised their arms in the Solidarity salute. Solidarity is much more than a protest for workers' rights; it is a spiritual expression rooted firmly in the church, which remains vibrant even in oppression. Joseph Stalin once mockingly dismissed the church's influence, asking how many divisions the Pope had. What would he say now to that remarkable gathering in Warsaw?

But another "visible effect," this one from Federico Fellini's award-winning film, *La Dolce Vita,* gives us a very different picture.

The movie opens with a view of Rome's magnificent skyline, the grand dome of St. Peter's in the center. A helicopter carrying a large object appears in the distance; as the camera zooms in, we see the object is a statue of Christ being hauled away from a downtown square. The camera then focuses on a group of young sunbathers who, distracted from their pleasure by the whirring blades, turn for a moment to mockery: "Why shouldn't Jesus take the bus like everyone else?" Then the helicopter flies on to discard its outdated cargo on a trash pile and the youngsters return to their worship in the sun.

That blasphemous scene, filmed in 1959, has proven to be all too prophetic. Today's Western culture rejects all absolutes and enshrines only self-indulgence. We put Jesus on the trash pile and worship the sun.

Make no mistake about it: the overriding struggle today is not economic, a tension between Marxism and capitalism, important as that is; it is not political, between the United States and the Soviets, or even between democracy and totalitarianism. It is, as it has been from the beginning, a spiritual battle between belief and unbelief—whether God is the alpha and the omega, sovereign Creator of heaven and earth, or whether, as Carl Sagan puts it, "the Cosmos is all that is or ever will be," and man therefore finds his ultimate destiny through himself.

The contrast between those scenes—the Warsaw mass and Fellini's film—tells an ironic and sad story. From Warsaw we learn that the Soviet juggernaut, with its awesome repression, its tanks and nuclear missiles, its constant barrage of antireligious propaganda, cannot erase the Gospel from the mind of Poland. But on the other side of the iron curtain, we are on the way to accomplishing the Soviet's task for them. What force cannot eradicate, we are happily discarding. Jesus is halfway to the trash pile.

Christians in Retreat

The hard truth is that despite the much-ballyhooed religious resurgence of the last decade, Christian values are in retreat. We Western Christians are losing the struggle for the hearts and minds of our neighbors.

We see this most obviously in the erosion of moral values—sexual permissiveness, the blatant parading of perversion, the continued casual disposal of unwanted unborn children, the breakup of the family, the consuming obsession with self and material acquisitions; or just look at crime for one example: we incarcerate more people per capita than any nation on earth, except for the Soviet Union and South Africa, yet our crime rate has soared. There are 100 times as many burglaries in "Christian" America as in so-called "pagan" Japan.

But if, as I have said, the battle is at root spiritual, these are merely the extreme symptoms of the disease—the rash which comes with a killing virus. Let's look at the root issue—how well is Christian truth permeating our national consciousness? Consider these facts:

• Less than 5 percent of the respondents in a 1981 *Psychology Today* survey considered moral or ethical issues significant when asked about their hopes and fears. (Concerns with a better standard of living scored 40 percent.)

• A 1979 *Christianity Today* survey revealed that only 26 percent of the general public believes Jesus

Christ to be fully God and fully man; among evangelicals the response climbed to only 43 percent.

• In a Gallup survey conducted for Dr. Robert Schuller, 81 percent of those polled said they considered themselves Christians. But only 42 percent knew Jesus delivered the Sermon on the Mount—and only 46 percent were able to name the four Gospels!

• Other Gallup polls reveal that in 1963, 65 percent of the American public believed the Bible to be infallible; but by 1982, that number declined to 37 percent.

• In another survey, 1,382 people were asked what they considered to be the book which had most influenced them. Fifteen cited the Bible—barely more than 1 percent.

We are called a "Christian" nation? For shame. We are a nation of biblical illiterates. The knowledge of God found in the Bible is the very foundation of any nation's Christian consensus. In the America of the '80s, it is being washed away; without it the house will not long stand.

Frontal Assaults

Why is the Christian worldview eroding in our nation?

The most obvious answer is the intense frontal assault waged against the Christian faith for the past quarter century. Under the guise of pluralism and civil liberty, the judiciary has rewritten the Constitution, interpreting freedom *of* religion to mean freedom *from* religion. Courts have ruled that nativity scenes, invocations, Christmas carols, voluntary prayers, and Bible study on public property threaten the constitutional rights of others. The Bible has been pushed out of public life altogether.

Infanticide, or abortion on demand, has been sanctioned by our nation's highest court. So have the rights of pornographers.

And in case you were wondering how the federal government officially views religion, I offer two opinions from the Supreme Court. The first, from 1933: "The essence of religion is belief in a relation to God involving duties superior to those arising from any human relation." I'll buy that. But during the turmoil of the '60s the Court saw fit to give us a new definition of religion: "A sincere and meaningful belief which occupies in the life of its possessor a place parallel to that filled by God of those admittedly qualifying for this [conscientious] exemption." In other words, in the eyes of the government, one certainly does not need God to be religious; if one is occupied by a sincere and meaningful belief in a tuna fish, perhaps, that will do just fine.

But whatever wounds our government has inflicted on Christian standards, they pale in comparison to the damage done by the media.

Network television bludgeons prime-time viewers with up to 38 violent acts per hour. Television executives—who say they are merely holding up a mirror to American society—give us a view of life 10 times more criminally violent than actual statistics. But if you tire of violence, you can tune in to your favorite brand of eroticism on the afternoon or evening soaps, including homosexual, bisexual, and even incestuous affairs.

Where, in this great wasteland, do we find any attempt to grapple with the truth? Where do we find even a hint of interest in prayer, in help from God? Is America really so godless as prime-time TV? Even on public TV, supposedly above the major networks' pandering to public taste, just when do we learn about the great Christian heritage of this nation and all Western civilization? The executives tell us there is not enough interest in these things to warrant the expense of production; tell me, when have they tried? For TV executives, apparently, Jesus is not on the way to the trash pile. He has been there for some time.

And the whole country is addicted. In 1977, a study conducted by the *Detroit Free Press* showed that adults as well as children, when cut off from TV, suffer symptoms similar to drug withdrawal. Significantly, 120 households were offered $500 to participate in the study, giving up 30 days of television. Only 27 accepted.

Christian philosopher Soren Kierkegaard was uncannily prophetic when more than a century ago he wrote, "Suppose someone invented an instrument, a convenient little talking tube, which could be heard over the whole land. I wonder if the police would forbid it fearing that the whole country would become mentally deranged if it were used."

But, startling as this may sound, these attacks are not really what concern me. I don't minimize them; of course they are grave. But they are also obvious. Many Christians are already sounding the alarm; and what's more, there is something we can do to fight back.

Where government officials push Christian values out of public life, we can live up to our duty as Christian citizens and push them back in. The Supreme Court has ruled that an unborn child has no rights, but we do not have to accept that as the final word. Christians must oppose it frontally, vigorously, and unceasingly. We must fight for a constitutional amendment to protect the unborn.

As for trash in films and TV, we are not helpless victims. TV executives do respond to pressure—particularly pressures of the marketplace. Turn the tube off and boycott the products of companies sponsoring trash. Support and encourage those who provide better fare, especially now that with the advent of cable TV the networks' monopoly is slipping away.

Sneak Attacks

But these frontal assaults are not my greatest concern; we may well win these battles and lose the war. Far more dangerous than the frontal assault is the sneak attack—the subtle, insidious invasion of secular values into the mainstream of American thought—and the church as well. We often do not even recognize these as attacks, and so fail to defend ourselves. As a culture, we're subtly manipulated by an interpretation here, a nuance there, the slant some journalist puts on the Christian message, the hidden agenda we don't discover until too late.

Let me offer some illustrations, all

from the media. The media have no monopoly on this kind of unconscious bias; I could cite the public schools, the courts, the textbooks on industrial management, or just about any source I wanted. But the media affect all of us very directly, and we all share in them. They provide the common ground of all members of our society. Therefore, consider these sneak attacks on our Christian values:

• *The media frame the issues in terms of thoroughly secularized questions.* Several years ago two Los Angeles doctors were accused of murder. They had removed the life support apparatus from a comatose man whose condition they diagnosed irreversible. First went the respirator; he began to breathe on his own. Then the doctors ceased intravenous feeding. Nine days later the man died—of starvation. NBC's anchorman pegged the story with the following: "The question of when to pull the plug may be about to get a thorough hearing in a Los Angeles courtroom."

When to pull the plug? What about *if?* The treatment of a dying man is full of ethical dilemmas. But are they all to be framed in terms of *when* to pull the plug? Have we already concluded that we must pull it? The anchorman's words suggest that the decision is merely complex, not agonizing. A cost-benefit analysis, which could be done on a computer, might resolve the moral questions. Convenience and productivity and overall cost determine who lives and who dies.

This is a scenario borrowed from the pages of Alexander Solzhenitsyn's *Cancer Ward.* For in the Soviet Union, where society is free from moral impediments, that is how decisions are made.

When we discover such things, we Christians tend to hurl invectives at the "satanic enemy" and claim it's all part of a sinister conspiracy. I overreacted in the same way during my White

House days when I believed the media distorted their coverage of Mr. Nixon to suit their own biases. But the fact is that secular journalists do not choose their words as part of some conscious plot to destroy Christian values. No, it's worse than that: the choice is unconscious, simply reflecting the worldview of the writer. The word "when" is what most naturally came to mind; to a Christian, the word "if" would be natural. Of course, that leads us to the real problem: you can count on one hand the Christians writing major news stories.

- *The media characterize the sides in terms that bias us toward or against their views.* Think how the simple choice of words can shape our thinking. Pro-abortionist groups, for example, stand for *free* choice; that's a good word. And they are "progressive" too (the assumption is anything new must be better) and are usually supported by the more "enlightened" elements of society. Anti-abortion groups, on the other hand, are against *free* choice, therefore regressive and usually religiously bigoted besides. The reader or viewer is influenced before the issue is even explained.

The December 1981 trial attacking the Arkansas statute which provided for teaching Creation in public schools offers another illustration. Consider the "objective" characterization of the two parties involved reported in the December 21, 1981 *Washington Post:* "The ACLU and the New York firm of Skadden Arps attacked the Arkansas law with a powerful case. Their brief is so good that there is talk of publishing it. Their witnesses gave brilliant little summaries of several fields of science, history, and religious philosophy." Such was the "enlightened" plaintiff.

The witnesses appearing in defense of the Creation theory, however, were "impassioned believers, rebellious educators, and scientific oddities. All but one of the Creation scientists came from obscure colleges or Bible schools. The one who didn't said he believed diseases dropped from space, that evolution caused Nazism, and that insects may be more intelligent than humans but are hiding their abilities." It goes on.

The point is simple. If you were an uninformed reader coming to this case, with whom would you ally yourself —the firm of Skadden Arps with its brilliant summaries, or the backwoods idiots from no-name colleges who probably still make live-animal sacrifices up in the hills when nobody is looking?

To sum up, in Arkansas, in December of 1981, to question evolutionary theory was to be stupid.

● *The media exile Christian concerns to strictly "religious programming."* A few years ago the late Christian thinker and writer, Francis Schaeffer, approached PBS about airing "How Shall We Then Live?" his excellent film series presenting a view of history, Creation, and the universe framed in the Judeo-Christian tradition. He was turned down cold—"too religious."

However, PBS happily aired "Cosmos," a sumptuous video science class which feeds the viewer a steady diet of "The Cosmos is all that is or ever will be." Apparently PBS executives believe they should not broadcast pro-Christian material, because that is too narrow. Anti-Christian material, on the other hand, is so broadly acceptable as to hardly be noticed. Unconsciously many viewers accept this; secularized society becomes "normal" to them.

Clearly the media has cast the Christian worldview as unworthy of prime-time review. This bias exiles Christianity to its own programming. It's good to have Christian programs, of course, but by compart-mentalizing us, keeping us in our own time slots, the media is in effect refusing to dignify the Christian view as a respectable alternative to the secular in the general marketplace.

There are many other press nuances which pass unnoticed but drive Christian truth out of mainstream thought.

When I speak to the media about my conversion, I *always* deliberately say "I accepted Jesus Christ"; but reporters will invariably translate that into my "religious conversion," or "conversion to Christianity," or even "born again," now that the term has been so secularized as to be harmless. How the world fears the person of Jesus Christ! Christianity? Fine. It preaches peace. But introduce a risen Lord who gives evidence that Carl Sagan's "Cosmos" is *not* all there is, and that arouses fierce antagonism.

One major American daily, in fact, refuses to use the word "Christ" when speaking about Jesus. To do so would be to make an editorial judgment.

- *The media misunderstand and misreport events with great Christian significance.* Since only 8 percent of secular reporters regularly attend church, it is not surprising that most fail to discern spiritual matters. Coverage of Pope John Paul's trip to Nicaragua is a clear example. The Pope stood alone on a platform to conduct mass while Sandinista officials held back the huge, friendly crowd, took over the front row seats and, for the benefit of the grinding TV cameras, shook their fists and screamed at the Pope. Each time they did so, the Pope lifted his crucifix over his head. A remarkable linguist, he conducted mass in the language of the Miskito Indians, thousands of whom the Sandinistas had ruthlessly murdered. Symbolically he conveyed the powerful truth: God offers grace to the people you killed. The crowd cheered, while the protesters howled with rage at the

Pope's open defiance.

It was a classic confrontation, reminding me of what historian Will Durant called the greatest drama of history—when Christ met Caesar in the arena—and Christ won. For without doubt, that unforgettable night in Managua, Christ won.

But what did American newsmen on the scene report of that classic confrontation? What did they see and hear? The Pope was inept and confused, they said, speaking in a language the crowd couldn't understand. And he failed to bring peace or healing to that troubled country. He berated Marxist priests and further divided his church.

Of course he did—and deliberately. He also indicted the Sandinistas for their massacres and their politicization of the church. He held up the indestructible truth of Christ against their shouted insults. But he did not achieve overnight reform; so the media labeled as "failure" what was in reality a truly heroic moment for Christians.

Subliminally, a nuance and a word at a time, the non-Christian perspective inexorably gains ground. If C.S. Lewis were alive today he might write of Screwtape's sad fate: Alas, he is among the unemployed; things are going quite nicely without his having to lift a finger.

The Enemy Inside

But now I must turn to the gravest concern of all. I have spoken of the frontal assaults and the sneak attacks. There is something worse to be considered. The enemy is in our midst. He has so infiltrated our camp that many simply no longer can tell an enemy from a friend, truth from heresy. We Christians cannot fight effectively against secularization because we are riddled with it ourselves.

In 1981, a very readable little book was published with the appealing title, *When Bad Things Happen to Good People.* Written by a Boston rabbi, Harold Kushner, it was an overnight sensation, 52 weeks on the *New York Times* bestseller list, millions of copies sold.

Kushner's thesis is simple enough: God is all-loving but not all-powerful; the bad things that happen to us are out of His control. So, the rabbi exhorts his readers to "learn to love and forgive Him [God] despite His limitations."

Now it will be immediately obvious to you that this god of Kushner's is not the God of Abraham and of Israel, not the all-powerful God revealed in the Scriptures.

But you may say, so what? If one rabbi rejects Jewish orthodoxy and writes a book offering easy answers to life's great mysteries and a hungry and hurting people gobble it up, what's the surprise?

Well, if that were the whole story, you'd be right. But there's more.

The book jacket carries the ringing endorsements of one of America's leading Christian personalities, as well as a seminary professor. It was widely distributed in Christian churches; in fact, I finally decided to read it only after a dozen or more evangelicals recommended it to me. Pastors preached from it. It was a big seller in many Christian bookstores.

When I looked around for critical comment I found only a few Christian publications negatively reviewing the book; others were silent. Even Rabbi Kushner said in a recent interview he was surprised his book had not received more criticism. When I wrote a critical article about the book for Prison Fellowship's newsletter, *Jubilee,* I was deluged with mail, most of it saying, "Amen, someone's finally speaking out." But several pastors angrily denounced me for challenging a book they had found "comforting" to their congregations.

"Comforting?" Indeed. So might doses of narcotics be comforting.

Kushner's book wasn't just the skewed theology of one rabbi; it was—and is—a national phenomenon, one of the most significant books in several years, enormously influencing our culture's perception of God. And we Christians went right along with the game, embracing it, even promoting it. My friends, that is not just buying into the errors of the secular culture; it is not a slight compromise with so-called realism. It is treachery to God; it is changing sides in the battle; it is promoting blasphemy.

And Kushner's book is not, I'm sorry to say, the only example. Whatever is hot in America's pop culture finds its way into the Christian market dressed in evangelical jargon. Many Christian "how-to" books, records, and tapes simply tell us how to use God as a lever to get whatever it is we desire. Get thin. Get successful. Get rich. Such religious adaptations of the self-indulgent, egocentric, materialistic culture are not only Jesus-justified hedonism but dreadful heresy—for they suggest that the majestic Creator God of this universe exists for man's pleasure rather than vice-versa.

So it is that we have, I fear, slipped unknowingly into a state of moral paralysis. We are so comfortable with the "comforting" world's ways we no longer are able to discern what is false and what is true. We have forgotten the words of Isaiah, "Woe to those who call evil good, and good evil" (5:20). We have forgotten that moral confusion is the enemy's favorite weapon.

For Satan comes not in a red suit carrying a pitchfork; rather, as Shakespeare wrote in *King Lear,* the devil is a gentleman. Before his fall he was called Lucifer, the angel of light and knowledge; in the Garden he was the most attractive of all the animals. And today he cloaks his propaganda in the conventional wisdom of the times—the rights of men and women to pursue the pleasure principle first articulated by John Stuart Mill. The pursuit of happiness, immediate and temporal, has become a moral obligation.

And the deceiver uses the bludgeon sparingly, preferring little subtleties, inferences, and suggestions which slip through the lines of Christian defenses, then over time establish themselves as legitimate. It's an insidious process of gradual compromise.

We live in an age in which compromise is applauded as one of the highest virtues of civilized men. Our pluralistic form of government uses compromise to make an issue acceptable to the greatest number of people by a process of negotiation. But what may occasionally work in the secular world is not necessarily

God's wisdom. A compromise of hot and cold yields lukewarm. And God, speaking in Revelation, is resolute about lukewarmness: "I know your deeds, that you are neither cold nor hot. . . . So because you are lukewarm, and neither hot nor cold, I will spit you out of my mouth" (3:15-16).

Who Will Prevail?

What then must we do? For the church as a whole there is required a massive reassertion of its biblical responsibilities. That is a huge task, larger than we can discuss here. But I have five specific exhortations:

1. *We must discern the false values of this world—and reject them.* The world wants quick-fix, easy answers, how to get whatever it wants at anyone's expense; that's why bestseller lists have for years been full of books like *Winning through Intimidation, Looking Out for*

Number One, Kushner's book, and the fad champion, *The One Minute Manager* (in 106 pages and for the princely sum of $15 you can get an instant course on guaranteed success). Now when these egocentric, success-at-any-price values invade Christian literature, creating a what's-in-it-for-me, God-will-shower-blessings-on-you gospel, we must jump off the bandwagon, rather than on. Instead, warn people of the pitfalls of this kind of cheap grace. And instead of puffy testimonies, every one with happy victorious endings, let's lead people to the real meat: the great classics by and about Augustine, Jonathan Edwards, John Calvin, Charles Spurgeon, Dietrich Bonhoeffer, C.S. Lewis or contemporaries like Francis Schaeffer, J.I. Packer, Malcolm Muggeridge, Carl Henry, and others of their caliber.

And we must have the courage to call heresy, heresy. Hard words, which are hard medicine, are needed.

2. *We must point people to the Holy Bible in their search for truth and answers.* We who follow Christ must take our stand the only place we can—on the holy, infallible Word of God. We don't have anything else.

I use the word "infallible" advisedly. There is no issue I've wrestled with harder since I've been a Christian than my view of the Scriptures. My lawyer's mind demanded evidence before I could believe the Bible to be without error. But the more I probed, the clearer that truth became. Ironically, it was as a result of my Watergate experiences that I became utterly convinced that the Bible is absolutely authoritative— God's inerrant revelation.

3. *We who are looked to by others for spiritual leadership must encourage disciplined Christian living.* Several years ago I had the opportunity to preach in the Full Gospel Church of Seoul, Korea. There were 10,000 people in the sanctuary,

15,000 in the overflow halls, six services on that Sunday. It was not the numbers which moved me; rather, I was overwhelmed by the presence of the Spirit. Afterward I told the pastor how excited I was about his church. He said, "Oh, this isn't the church; this is just where we gather Sunday morning. The church, you see, is in the home—10,000 homes all across Seoul where members meet every morning for two hours of Bible study and prayer." Korean Christians wouldn't think of beginning their day without earnest prayer and study of the Word of God.

Then I understood why in that country of 35 million Buddhists and only 2 million evangelical Christians, Christian values dominate the culture. It is because Korean Christians take their faith seriously. We in this supposedly Christian nation, but one in which humanist values dominate, desperately need to learn from our Korean brothers and sisters. We need to get cheap grace out of our churches, and get people into the Word of God and serious, disciplined prayer.

4. *We must equip the laity to take the Gospel into the world.* This is the major reason I wrote my third book, *Loving God:* to equip the ordinary Christian to understand, to defend, and to articulate the basic truths of his faith; and to live that faith courageously in the world.

Ask any layman today what his ministry is, and he will say, "It's Gideons on Thursday night," or "It's a church committee." That's all fine, of course, but the layman is called to go *out* of the church, to *be* a witness for Jesus Christ in his home, job, country club, wherever he is, 24 hours a day. Jay Kesler, president of Taylor University, says the church today is like a pro football game: 100,000 people sitting in the stands watching 22 men on the field beating themselves to a pulp. True Christianity is not a spectator sport; it is not to be sat out in church pews; it is to be lived out in the world so that "the blessings of God might show forth in every area of life" as the great Puritan pastor Cotton Mather put it.

And holy living isn't just personal piety; it is standing for justice and righteousness in society. We can't pay someone else to do that; we don't get off the hook by tithing or paying dues to some moralistic organization. God calls each of us to live it out ourselves. That can be painful and bloody; usually it means getting our hands dirty. Always there is a cost.

5. *We must get off the defensive.* We must not simply sit in our bunkers waiting to repel the secular invaders; instead let us take our message boldly into the secular marketplace.

Just before a governor's prayer breakfast where I was to speak, the chairman asked me not to mention the name of Jesus Christ because there were Jews in the audience. You know what to do with advice like that—and that's what I did. The first people to thank me afterward were Jewish. Don't ever water down your message for anyone.

We need to stop talking to ourselves and speak instead to the secular world. There is real hunger out there. John Wesley said the "way to a man's heart is through his mind," so we need to be giving quality Christian literature to our non-Christian neighbors. My own Christian life began because a Christian friend handed me *Mere Christianity.*

And let's get our skilled young people into ABC, NBC, and CBS newsrooms.

Finally, let us not only speak but demonstrate what the Gospel means when it is lived out in the secular marketplace. Whenever Prison Fellowship does a community service project, taking inmates out of prison, housing them with volunteers, and putting them to work weatherizing a widow's home or working with the poor, the media covers it. It is, thus, a witness which invades the secular marketplace. People who would never go into church can *see* that Christianity makes a difference in the lives of people in their community.

There are countless ways we can do this if only we have the will and courage to get up out of our comfortable pews and take our message into the world, doing battle for the hearts and minds of mankind.

What of the future? Can we prevail in the great ideological struggle of the 20th century? For at least 20 years the Christian worldview, which has historically provided the moral undergirding of this nation, has been slowly giving ground to steadily advancing forces of humanism and nihilism. By what heroic effort can the tide of battle be turned?

Some may well conclude that I belong in the ranks of those who see only an apocalyptic vision of the future. Indeed, if our destiny depended on the weapons of this world, I would be an incurable pessimist. But my view is best expressed by the closing words of one of those classics of Christian literature I alluded to earlier. In *Real Christianity,* written late in the 18th century and republished in modern English by Multnomah Press, the great Christian parliamentarian and abolitionist leader, William Wilberforce, looked at the world around him. It was a grim picture: Europe awash in tidal waves of humanism caused by the French Revolution, and in England, as Wilberforce wrote, "Infidelity has lifted up her head without shame." But he concluded: "I must confess equally boldly that my own solid hopes for the well-being of my country depend, not so much on her navies and armies, nor on the wisdom of her rulers, nor on the spirit of her people, as on the persuasion that she still contains many who love and obey the Gospel of Christ. I believe that their prayers may yet prevail."

There soon followed one of the great revivals of modern time. So too is it my belief that the prayers and work of those who love and obey Christ in our world may yet prevail.